INTERDISCIPLINARY APPROACH TO RESPIRATORY CARE

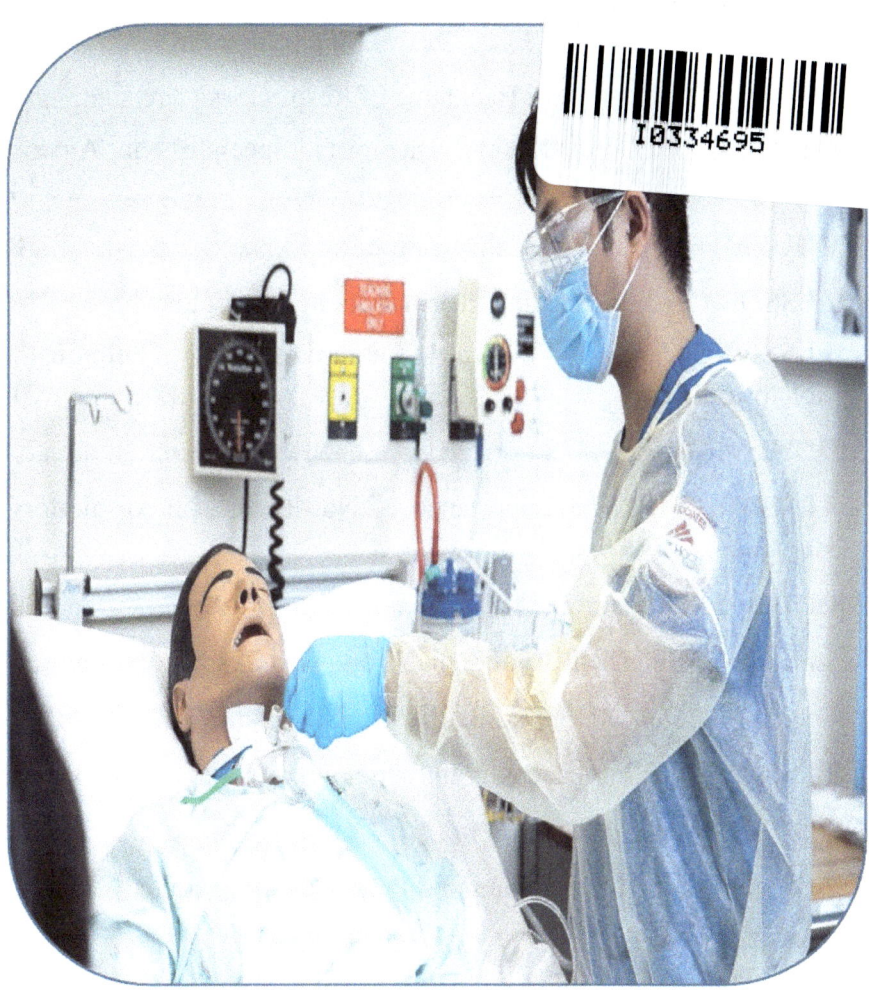

TABLE OF CONTENTS

INTRODUCTION 2
MODULE ONE 3
   LESSON ONE: Interdisciplinary Respiratory Care 3
   LESSON TWO: The Role of Physicians in Respiratory Care 7
Module two 11
   Lesson one: Nurses: The Backbone of Respiratory Care 11
   LESSON TWO: Respiratory Therapists: Specialists in Airway Management 14
MODULE THREE 18
   LESSON ONE: Integrating Pharmacists in Respiratory Care 18
   LESSON TWO: Physical Therapists and Pulmonary Rehabilitation 21
MODULE FOUR 26
   LESSON ONE: The Importance of Nutritionists in Respiratory Health 26
MODULE FIVE 30
   LESSON ONE: The Role of Social Workers in Respiratory Care .. 30
MODULE SIX 34
   LESSON ONE: Implementing Interdisciplinary Care in Practice ... 34
MODULE seven 39
   LESSON ONE: Case Studies and Practical Applications 39
CONCLUSION 44
REFERENCES 45

COURSE OVERVIEW

This course provides a comprehensive exploration of interdisciplinary respiratory care, emphasizing collaboration, communication, and evidence-based practice. Participants will gain a deep understanding of the roles and responsibilities of various healthcare professionals in managing respiratory conditions and learn how to effectively integrate their expertise to optimize patient outcomes.

COURSE OBJECTIVE

By the end of this course, participants will be able to explain the anatomical and physiological principles underlying respiratory function and their relevance to interdisciplinary care. Identify the roles and responsibilities of physicians, nurses, respiratory therapists, pharmacists, physical therapists, nutritionists, and social workers in interdisciplinary respiratory care teams. Evaluate pharmacotherapeutic interventions for respiratory conditions and their impact on patient management within interdisciplinary care settings. Through a combination of didactic instruction, interactive discussions, and hands-on activities, participants will emerge from this course equipped with the knowledge, skills, and confidence to contribute effectively to interdisciplinary respiratory care teams and enhance the quality of care for patients with respiratory conditions.

COURSE MATERIALS

To learn this course, **healthcare providers/ participants** must be provided with materials like a Pen, pencil, notebook, and notepad to better understand and make it easy for them to learn.

INTRODUCTION

Respiratory care is a critical component of healthcare that spans across various specialties. The lungs and respiratory system are vital for life, and their care requires a nuanced, multifaceted approach. "Breathing Together: An Interdisciplinary Approach to Respiratory Care" aims to bridge the gaps between different healthcare providers, fostering a collaborative environment that enhances patient outcomes. This book is designed for healthcare providers who seek to deepen their understanding of respiratory care from an interdisciplinary perspective.

The modern healthcare landscape is increasingly complex, necessitating a collaborative approach to patient care. No single healthcare professional can address all the needs of patients with respiratory issues. Physicians, nurses, respiratory therapists, pharmacists, physical therapists, and nutritionists all play integral roles. Each discipline brings unique expertise and perspectives, making it crucial to understand how they can work together effectively.

The interdisciplinary approach to respiratory care is not just a theoretical concept but a practical necessity. For instance, a patient with chronic obstructive pulmonary disease (COPD) may require the expertise of a physician for diagnosis and treatment planning, a nurse for ongoing monitoring and patient education, a respiratory therapist for airway management and mechanical ventilation, a pharmacist for medication management, a physical therapist for pulmonary rehabilitation, and a nutritionist to ensure optimal dietary support. By working together, these professionals can provide comprehensive care that addresses all aspects of the patient's condition.

MODULE ONE

LESSON ONE: INTERDISCIPLINARY RESPIRATORY CARE

The concept of interdisciplinary respiratory care has gained significant traction in recent years, driven by the recognition that complex health issues require a coordinated approach. This lesson will provide a comprehensive introduction to the interdisciplinary model, defining its key components and emphasizing its importance in the realm of respiratory care.

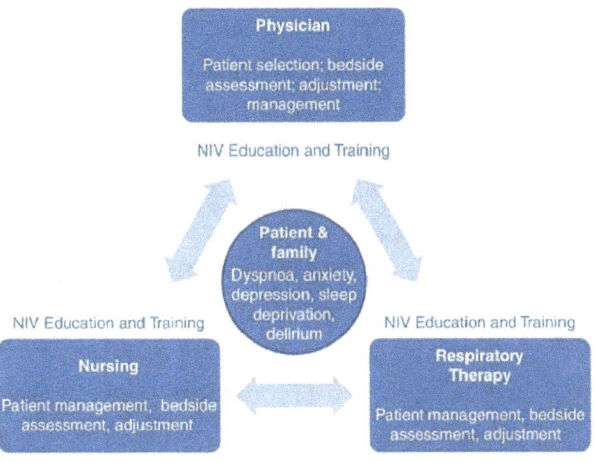

Understanding Interdisciplinary Care

Interdisciplinary care involves the collaboration of professionals from different disciplines working together towards a common goal. In respiratory care, this means bringing together physicians, nurses, respiratory therapists, pharmacists, physical therapists, and nutritionists to address the multifaceted needs of patients with respiratory conditions.

The Evolution of Respiratory Care

Historically, respiratory care was often viewed as the sole responsibility of physicians and respiratory therapists. However, as our understanding of respiratory diseases and their management has evolved, so has the recognition of the need for a more holistic approach. The emergence of chronic diseases like COPD, asthma, and interstitial lung diseases, which require long-term management and diverse interventions, has underscored the necessity for interdisciplinary collaboration.

Key Components of Interdisciplinary Respiratory Care

- Collaborative Practice: At the heart of interdisciplinary care is the concept of collaborative practice. This involves open communication, mutual respect, and shared decision-making among all team members. Each professional brings a unique set of skills and knowledge, contributing to a more comprehensive care plan.
- Patient-Centered Care: Interdisciplinary care places the patient at the center of the healthcare delivery model. This means understanding the patient's needs, preferences, and values, and involving them in their care decisions. Patient education and empowerment are crucial components of this approach.
- Integrated Care Plans: Effective interdisciplinary care requires the development of integrated care plans that incorporate input from all relevant disciplines. These plans are dynamic and adapt to the changing needs of the patient.
- Continuous Communication: Regular communication among team members is essential to ensure continuity of care and to address any emerging issues promptly. This can be facilitated through regular meetings, shared electronic health records, and other communication tools.

Benefits of Interdisciplinary Respiratory Care

Improved Patient Outcomes: Studies have shown that interdisciplinary care can lead to better health outcomes, including reduced hospital admissions, shorter hospital stays, and improved quality of life for patients with chronic respiratory diseases.

- Enhanced Patient Satisfaction: Patients often report higher levels of satisfaction with their care when they perceive that

their healthcare providers are working together cohesively and addressing their needs comprehensively.
- Professional Development: For healthcare providers, working in an interdisciplinary team can enhance professional development by providing opportunities to learn from colleagues in different disciplines and to develop a broader understanding of patient care.

Challenges and Barriers

Despite its benefits, implementing an interdisciplinary approach to respiratory care can be challenging. Some of the common barriers include:

- Lack of Training: Healthcare professionals may not receive adequate training in interdisciplinary practice during their education.
- Communication Issues: Differences in terminology, communication styles, and professional cultures can hinder effective collaboration.
- Administrative Hurdles: Coordinating care across different disciplines and healthcare settings can be logistically complex and time-consuming.

Moving Forward

To overcome these challenges, healthcare organizations must prioritize interdisciplinary education and training, foster a culture of collaboration, and invest in systems and tools that facilitate communication and coordination.

Interdisciplinary respiratory care represents a paradigm shift in how we approach the management of respiratory diseases. By leveraging the strengths and expertise of diverse healthcare professionals, we can provide more comprehensive, patient-centered care that improves outcomes and enhances the patient experience.

DISCUSSION QUESTIONS

- How does a deep understanding of respiratory anatomy and physiology contribute to the development of effective interdisciplinary care plans for patients with respiratory conditions?
- What are some common respiratory disorders, and how do they affect the anatomy and physiology of the respiratory system?

LESSON TWO: THE ROLE OF PHYSICIANS IN RESPIRATORY CARE

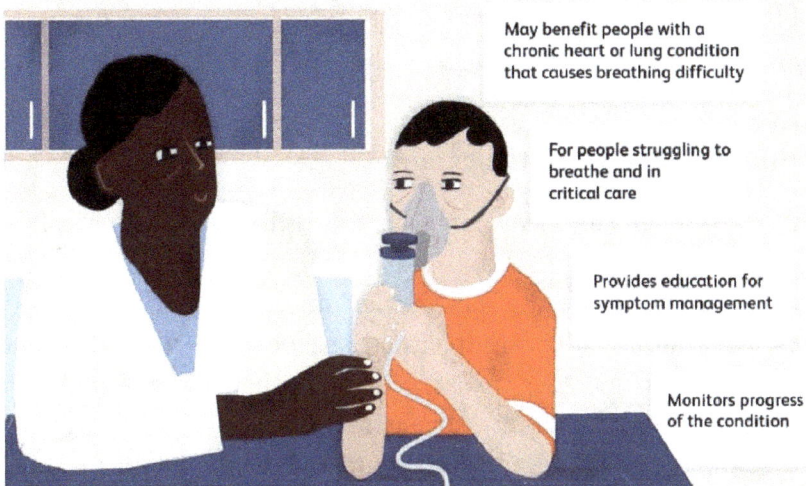

Physicians play a pivotal role in the interdisciplinary approach to respiratory care. As primary decision-makers in the diagnosis and treatment of respiratory conditions, their expertise and leadership are crucial. This lesson explores the various responsibilities of physicians in respiratory care, highlighting their interactions with other healthcare professionals and their contributions to a collaborative care model.

Diagnostic Expertise

Physicians, particularly pulmonologists, are responsible for diagnosing respiratory conditions. This involves taking detailed patient histories, performing physical examinations, and ordering and interpreting diagnostic tests such as spirometry, chest X-rays, CT scans, and blood gas analyses. Accurate diagnosis is the first step in developing an effective treatment plan and requires a deep understanding of respiratory physiology and pathology.

Treatment Planning and Management

Once a diagnosis is made, physicians develop and oversee the implementation of a treatment plan. This may include prescribing medications, recommending lifestyle changes, and coordinating with other healthcare providers for interventions such as pulmonary rehabilitation and nutritional support. Physicians must stay abreast of the latest research and treatment guidelines to provide evidence-based care.

Coordination and Communication

Effective communication and coordination with other members of the healthcare team are essential in the interdisciplinary model. Physicians must ensure that all relevant information is shared with nurses, respiratory therapists, pharmacists, physical therapists, and nutritionists. This includes updating them on the patient's condition, treatment progress, and any changes in the care plan. Regular interdisciplinary meetings and case conferences are vital for fostering collaboration and ensuring that all team members are aligned in their approach to patient care.

Patient Education and Empowerment

Physicians also play a key role in patient education. They must explain the diagnosis, treatment options, and prognosis to the patient and their family, ensuring they understand the importance of adherence to the treatment plan. Empowering patients through education can enhance their engagement in their care and improve outcomes. Physicians often work with nurses and other team members to provide comprehensive education and support.

Advanced Interventions and Procedures

In many cases, physicians are responsible for performing advanced interventions and procedures. These may include bronchoscopy, thoracentesis, or managing patients on mechanical ventilation. Physicians must have the necessary skills and experience to perform these procedures safely and effectively. They also play a critical role in managing complications and making decisions about the escalation or de-escalation of care.

Research and Continuous Improvement

Physicians are often involved in research and quality improvement initiatives aimed at advancing the field of respiratory care. This includes conducting clinical trials, publishing research findings, and implementing evidence-based practices within their healthcare institutions. By contributing to the body of knowledge in respiratory medicine, physicians help to improve care standards and patient outcomes.

Collaboration with Other Specialists

In complex cases, physicians may need to collaborate with other specialists, such as cardiologists, infectious disease experts, or thoracic surgeons. Effective interdisciplinary care requires seamless communication and coordination with these specialists to address all aspects of the patient's health.

Challenges Faced By Physicians

Despite their critical role, physicians face several challenges in the interdisciplinary care model. These include:

- Time Constraints: Balancing clinical responsibilities with administrative tasks and interdisciplinary meetings can be demanding.
- Resource Limitations: Limited access to certain diagnostic tools or treatments can hinder the ability to provide optimal care.
- Systemic Barriers: Bureaucratic and systemic issues, such as insurance approvals and hospital policies, can complicate the coordination of care.

Enhancing Physician Involvement in Interdisciplinary Care

To enhance the role of physicians in interdisciplinary respiratory care, several strategies can be implemented:

- Interdisciplinary Training: Providing physicians with training in interdisciplinary practice during their medical education and continuing education programs can improve their ability to work effectively in a team.
- Support Systems: Implementing support systems, such as dedicated care coordinators and administrative assistants, can help manage the logistical aspects of interdisciplinary care.
- Technology Integration: Utilizing technology, such as electronic health records and telemedicine, can facilitate communication and coordination among team members.

Physicians are integral to the interdisciplinary approach to respiratory care. Their expertise in diagnosis, treatment planning, and advanced interventions, combined with their ability to coordinate and communicate with other healthcare providers, is essential for delivering comprehensive, patient-centered care. By addressing the challenges they face and enhancing their involvement in interdisciplinary practice, we can improve outcomes for patients with respiratory conditions.

DISCUSSION QUESTIONS

- What are the key principles that guide interdisciplinary practice in respiratory care, and how do they promote better patient outcomes?
- How can healthcare organizations foster a culture of collaboration and communication among interdisciplinary team members in respiratory care settings?

MODULE TWO

LESSON ONE: NURSES: THE BACKBONE OF RESPIRATORY CARE

Nurses play a fundamental role in the interdisciplinary team, providing continuous care and support to patients with respiratory conditions. This lesson delves into the responsibilities and contributions of nurses in respiratory care, highlighting their critical role in patient monitoring, education, and coordination.

Patient Monitoring and Assessment

Nurses are often the first point of contact for patients and play a crucial role in monitoring and assessing their respiratory status. This includes measuring vital signs, observing respiratory patterns, and identifying early signs of respiratory distress. Nurses use their clinical judgment to assess the effectiveness of treatments and interventions, providing valuable feedback to the rest of the healthcare team.

Administering Treatments and Medications

Nurses are responsible for administering medications and treatments prescribed by physicians. This includes delivering bronchodilators, steroids, antibiotics, and other respiratory medications. They must be knowledgeable about the indications, dosages, and potential side effects of these medications to ensure safe and effective administration.

Patient Education and Advocacy

Educating patients about their respiratory condition and the importance of adherence to their treatment plan is a key responsibility of nurses. They provide instructions on medication use, inhaler techniques, breathing exercises, and lifestyle modifications. Nurses also advocate for patients, ensuring their needs and preferences are considered in the care plan.

Coordination of Care

Nurses play a central role in coordinating care among different healthcare providers. They communicate with physicians, respiratory therapists, pharmacists, and other team members to ensure that all aspects of the patient's care are addressed. This coordination is essential for providing seamless, integrated care.

Providing Emotional Support

Living with a respiratory condition can be challenging for patients and their families. Nurses provide emotional support, helping patients cope with anxiety, fear, and depression. They offer a compassionate presence and listen to patients' concerns, building trusting relationships that enhance the overall care experience.

Implementing Care Plans

Nurses are responsible for implementing care plans developed by the interdisciplinary team. This includes performing respiratory assessments, monitoring oxygen therapy, and assisting with pulmonary rehabilitation exercises. Nurses ensure that care plans are followed accurately and make adjustments as needed based on the patient's response.

Documentation and Reporting

Accurate documentation and reporting are critical aspects of nursing practice. Nurses maintain detailed records of patient assessments, treatments, and responses to interventions. This documentation is essential for ensuring continuity of care and for legal and regulatory purposes.

Challenges Faced by Nurses

Nurses face several challenges in their role within the interdisciplinary team:

- Workload and Staffing Issues: High patient-to-nurse ratios and staffing shortages can impact the quality of care.
- Complex Cases: Managing patients with complex respiratory conditions requires specialized knowledge and skills.
- Emotional Toll: Providing care for critically ill patients can be emotionally taxing.

Enhancing the Role of Nurses in Interdisciplinary Care

To enhance the role of nurses in interdisciplinary respiratory care, the following strategies can be implemented:

- Ongoing Education and Training: Providing nurses with continuing education and training in respiratory care can enhance their knowledge and skills.
- Supportive Work Environment: Creating a supportive work environment with adequate staffing and resources can help nurses manage their workload and provide high-quality care.
- Interdisciplinary Collaboration: Encouraging regular interdisciplinary meetings and communication can foster a collaborative culture and improve care coordination.

Nurses are the backbone of respiratory care, providing essential monitoring, treatment, education, and support to patients. Their role in the interdisciplinary team is vital for delivering comprehensive, patient-centered care. By addressing the challenges they face and enhancing their involvement in interdisciplinary practice, we can improve outcomes for patients with respiratory conditions.

DISCUSSION QUESTIONS

- What specific roles and responsibilities do physicians play in interdisciplinary respiratory care teams, and how do these roles differ from other healthcare professionals?
- How can physicians effectively collaborate with other members of the interdisciplinary team to ensure comprehensive care for patients with respiratory conditions?

LESSON TWO: RESPIRATORY THERAPISTS: SPECIALISTS IN AIRWAY MANAGEMENT

Respiratory therapists (RTs) are essential members of the interdisciplinary team, specializing in airway management and mechanical ventilation. This lesson explores the unique contributions of respiratory therapists in

Airway Management Team
A Multidisciplinary Approach

- ER- MD/RN
- ICU- Surgical/Medical/Neuro
- Acute Care Surgery
- Anesthesia
- Otolaryngology
- Cardiology
- Gastroenterology
- Interventional Radiology
- Clinical Nurse Specialists
- Pharmacy
- Respiratory Therapy
- Rapid Response Team
- Transitional Resident
- Medical Student
- Quality/Risk

respiratory care, highlighting their expertise in managing complex respiratory conditions and their collaboration with other healthcare providers.

Expertise in Airway Management

Respiratory therapists are trained in advanced airway management techniques, including intubation, extubation, and tracheostomy care. They are skilled in assessing and maintaining airway patency, ensuring that patients receive adequate ventilation and oxygenation.

Mechanical Ventilation

One of the primary responsibilities of respiratory therapists is managing mechanical ventilation for patients with respiratory failure. This includes setting up and adjusting ventilator settings, monitoring ventilator parameters, and troubleshooting issues. RTs work closely with physicians to optimize ventilator management and wean patients from mechanical ventilation when appropriate.

Administering Respiratory Therapies

Respiratory therapists administer a variety of respiratory therapies, including bronchodilators, mucolytics, and chest physiotherapy. They are knowledgeable about the indications, mechanisms of action, and potential side effects of these therapies, ensuring that they are delivered safely and effectively.

Conducting Diagnostic Tests

RTs perform and interpret diagnostic tests such as arterial blood gases (ABGs), pulmonary function tests (PFTs), and sleep studies. These tests provide critical information about the patient's respiratory status and help guide treatment decisions.

Patient and Family Education

Educating patients and their families about respiratory conditions and treatments is a key responsibility of respiratory therapists. They provide instructions on the use of inhalers, nebulizers, and other respiratory devices, as well as breathing exercises and techniques to manage symptoms.

Collaboration with the Healthcare Team

Respiratory therapists collaborate with physicians, nurses, pharmacists, and other healthcare providers to develop and implement comprehensive care plans. Their expertise in respiratory care is essential for ensuring that all aspects of the patient's respiratory needs are addressed.

Research and Quality Improvement

Many respiratory therapists are involved in research and quality improvement initiatives aimed at advancing respiratory care practices. This includes participating in clinical trials, implementing evidence-based practices, and contributing to the development of clinical guidelines.

Challenges Faced by Respiratory Therapists

RTs face several challenges in their role within the interdisciplinary team:

- Complex Patient Care: Managing patients with complex respiratory conditions requires specialized skills and knowledge.
- Technological Advances: Keeping up with advancements in respiratory care technology and equipment can be challenging.
- Interdisciplinary Communication: Ensuring effective communication and collaboration with other healthcare providers is essential but can be difficult to achieve.

Enhancing the Role of Respiratory Therapists in Interdisciplinary Care

To enhance the role of respiratory therapists in interdisciplinary respiratory care, the following strategies can be implemented:

- Ongoing Education and Training: Providing RTs with continuing education and training in respiratory care and interdisciplinary practice can enhance their knowledge and skills.
- Supportive Work Environment: Creating a supportive work environment with adequate resources and opportunities for professional development can help RTs manage their workload and provide high-quality care.
- Interdisciplinary Collaboration: Encouraging regular interdisciplinary meetings and communication can foster a collaborative culture and improve care coordination.

Respiratory therapists are specialists in airway management and mechanical ventilation, playing a critical role in the interdisciplinary team. Their expertise in managing complex respiratory conditions and their collaboration with other healthcare providers are essential for delivering comprehensive, patient-centered care. By addressing the challenges they face and enhancing their involvement in interdisciplinary practice, we can improve outcomes for patients with respiratory conditions.

DISCUSSION QUESTIONS

- How do respiratory therapists contribute to the management of respiratory conditions, particularly in critical care settings, and what specialized skills do they bring to the interdisciplinary team?
- What are some challenges respiratory therapists may face in their role within the interdisciplinary team, and how can these challenges be addressed to optimize patient care?

MODULE THREE

LESSON ONE: INTEGRATING PHARMACISTS IN RESPIRATORY CARE

Pharmacists are vital members of the interdisciplinary respiratory care team, contributing their expertise in medication management and patient education. This lesson explores the role of pharmacists in respiratory care, highlighting their contributions to optimizing pharmacotherapy and enhancing patient outcomes.

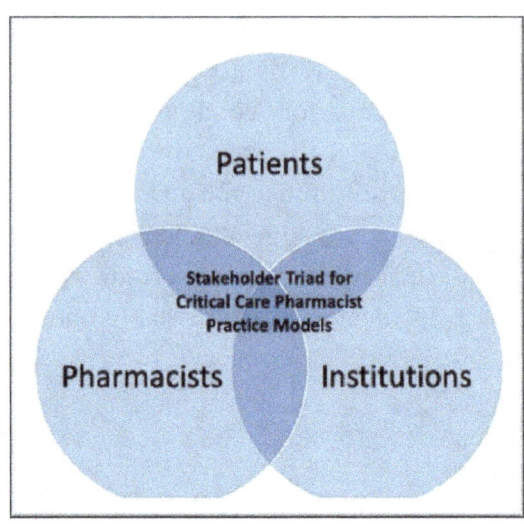

Expertise in Medication Management

Pharmacists are experts in pharmacotherapy, with a deep understanding of the medications used to treat respiratory conditions. This includes bronchodilators, corticosteroids, antibiotics, mucolytics, and other respiratory medications. Pharmacists ensure that medications are used safely and effectively, taking into account the patient's medical history, comorbidities, and potential drug interactions.

Medication Reconciliation

Pharmacists play a critical role in medication reconciliation, ensuring that patients' medication lists are accurate and up-to-date. This is particularly important for patients with respiratory conditions, who often take multiple medications. Pharmacists review medication lists, identify discrepancies, and work with the healthcare team to resolve any issues.

Patient Education and Counseling

Educating patients about their medications is a key responsibility of pharmacists. This includes explaining the purpose, dosing, and potential side effects of each medication, as well as providing instructions on how to use inhalers, nebulizers, and other respiratory devices. Pharmacists also counsel patients on adherence to their medication regimen and strategies to manage side effects.

Monitoring and Adjusting Therapy

Pharmacists monitor patients' responses to medications and collaborate with physicians and other healthcare providers to adjust therapy as needed. This may involve changing dosages, switching medications, or adding new treatments. Pharmacists use their expertise to optimize pharmacotherapy and improve patient outcomes.

Drug Formulary Management

Pharmacists are involved in managing the drug formulary, ensuring that the most effective and cost-efficient medications are available for treating respiratory conditions. They evaluate new medications and make recommendations for inclusion in the formulary based on evidence of safety, efficacy, and cost-effectiveness.

Research and Quality Improvement

Many pharmacists are involved in research and quality improvement initiatives aimed at advancing respiratory care practices. This includes conducting clinical trials, implementing evidence-based practices, and contributing to the development of clinical guidelines.

Collaboration with the Healthcare Team

Pharmacists collaborate with physicians, nurses, respiratory therapists, and other healthcare providers to develop and implement comprehensive care plans. Their expertise in medication management is essential for ensuring that all aspects of the patient's pharmacotherapy are addressed.

Challenges Faced by Pharmacists

Pharmacists face several challenges in their role within the interdisciplinary team:

- Complex Medication Regimens: Managing complex medication regimens for patients with respiratory conditions requires specialized knowledge and skills.
- Resource Limitations: Limited access to certain medications and resources can hinder the ability to provide optimal care.
- Interdisciplinary Communication: Ensuring effective communication and collaboration with other healthcare providers is essential but can be difficult to achieve.

Enhancing the Role of Pharmacists in Interdisciplinary Care

To enhance the role of pharmacists in interdisciplinary respiratory care, the following strategies can be implemented:

- Ongoing Education and Training: Providing pharmacists with continuing education and training in respiratory care and interdisciplinary practice can enhance their knowledge and skills.
- Supportive Work Environment: Creating a supportive work environment with adequate resources and opportunities for professional development can help pharmacists manage their workload and provide high-quality care.
- Interdisciplinary Collaboration: Encouraging regular interdisciplinary meetings and communication can foster a collaborative culture and improve care coordination.

Pharmacists are vital members of the interdisciplinary respiratory care team, contributing their expertise in medication management and patient education. Their role in optimizing pharmacotherapy and enhancing patient outcomes is essential for delivering comprehensive, patient-centered care. By addressing the challenges they face and enhancing their involvement in interdisciplinary practice, we can improve outcomes for patients with respiratory conditions.

DISCUSSION QUESTIONS

- What are the specific challenges pharmacists face in managing medications for patients with respiratory conditions within interdisciplinary teams, and how can these challenges be mitigated?
- How can pharmacists contribute to the development and implementation of evidence-based guidelines for pharmacotherapy in respiratory care, and what impact does this collaboration have on patient outcomes?

LESSON TWO: PHYSICAL THERAPISTS AND PULMONARY REHABILITATION

Physical therapists (PTs) are essential members of the interdisciplinary team, specializing in pulmonary rehabilitation and improving the physical function and quality of life of patients with respiratory conditions. This lesson explores

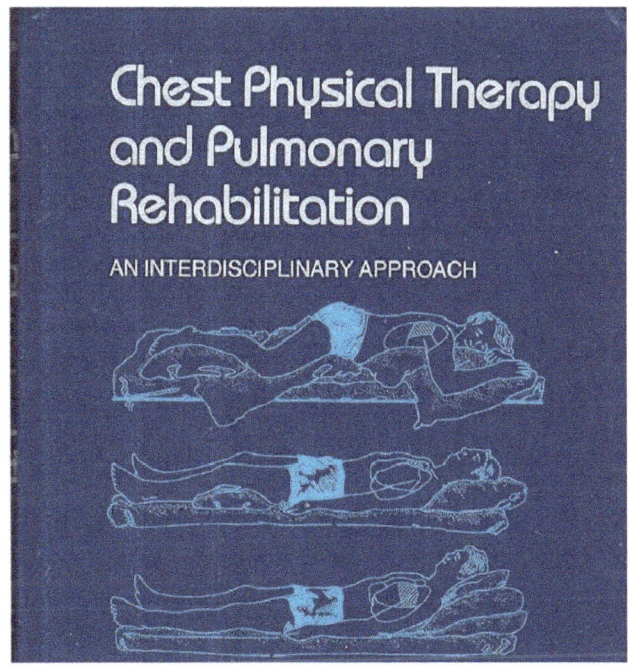

the role of physical therapists in respiratory care, highlighting their contributions to pulmonary rehabilitation and their collaboration with other healthcare providers.

Expertise in Pulmonary Rehabilitation

Physical therapists are trained in the principles and practices of pulmonary rehabilitation, a comprehensive intervention designed to improve the physical and psychological well-being of patients with chronic respiratory diseases. This includes exercise training, education, and behavior change aimed at improving the patient's functional status and quality of life.

Exercise Training

One of the primary components of pulmonary rehabilitation is exercise training. Physical therapists design and supervise individualized exercise programs that include aerobic, strength, and flexibility exercises. These programs are tailored to the patient's needs, abilities, and limitations, and are aimed at improving respiratory muscle strength, endurance, and overall physical fitness.

Breathing Techniques

Physical therapists teach patients various breathing techniques to improve ventilation and reduce breathlessness. These techniques include diaphragmatic breathing, pursed-lip breathing, and paced breathing. PTs work with patients to practice these techniques and incorporate them into their daily activities.

Education and Self-Management

Educating patients about their respiratory condition and the importance of physical activity is a key responsibility of physical therapists. They provide information on the benefits of exercise, strategies to manage symptoms, and techniques to conserve energy. PTs also empower patients to take an active role in their care through self-management education.

Monitoring and Progression

Physical therapists monitor patients' progress throughout the pulmonary rehabilitation program, adjusting the exercise regimen as needed to ensure optimal outcomes. This includes tracking improvements in exercise capacity, respiratory function, and quality of life. PTs use objective measures such as the six-minute walk test (6MWT) and spirometry to assess progress.

Collaboration with the Healthcare Team

Physical therapists collaborate with physicians, nurses, respiratory therapists, and other healthcare providers to develop and implement comprehensive care plans. Their expertise in pulmonary rehabilitation is essential for ensuring that all aspects of the patient's physical function are addressed.

Research and Quality Improvement

Many physical therapists are involved in research and quality improvement initiatives aimed at advancing pulmonary rehabilitation practices. This includes conducting clinical trials, implementing evidence-based practices, and contributing to the development of clinical guidelines.

Challenges Faced by Physical Therapists

Physical therapists face several challenges in their role within the interdisciplinary team:

- Patient Adherence: Ensuring that patients adhere to the exercise program and other rehabilitation components can be challenging, especially for those with severe respiratory limitations.
- Resource Limitations: Limited access to rehabilitation facilities and equipment can hinder the ability to provide optimal care.

- Complex Cases: Managing patients with multiple comorbidities and varying levels of physical function requires specialized skills and adaptability.

Enhancing the Role of Physical Therapists in Interdisciplinary Care

To enhance the role of physical therapists in interdisciplinary respiratory care, the following strategies can be implemented:

- Ongoing Education and Training: Providing PTs with continuing education and training in pulmonary rehabilitation and interdisciplinary practice can enhance their knowledge and skills.
- Supportive Work Environment: Creating a supportive work environment with adequate resources and opportunities for professional development can help PTs manage their workload and provide high-quality care.
- Interdisciplinary Collaboration: Encouraging regular interdisciplinary meetings and communication can foster a collaborative culture and improve care coordination.

Physical therapists are essential members of the interdisciplinary respiratory care team, specializing in pulmonary rehabilitation and improving the physical function and quality of life of patients with respiratory conditions. Their expertise in exercise training, breathing techniques, and patient education is vital for delivering comprehensive, patient-centered care. By addressing the challenges they face and enhancing their involvement in interdisciplinary practice, we can improve outcomes for patients with respiratory conditions.

DISCUSSION QUESTIONS

- What are the unique contributions of physical therapists to pulmonary rehabilitation programs, and how do these contributions improve respiratory outcomes for patients?

- How can physical therapists collaborate with other members of the interdisciplinary team to ensure a holistic approach to respiratory care, particularly in the context of pulmonary rehabilitation?

MODULE FOUR

LESSON ONE: THE IMPORTANCE OF NUTRITIONISTS IN RESPIRATORY HEALTH

Nutritionists play a crucial role in the interdisciplinary team, contributing their expertise in dietary management to support respiratory health. This lesson explores the role of nutritionists in respiratory care, highlighting their contributions to optimizing nutrition and enhancing patient outcomes.

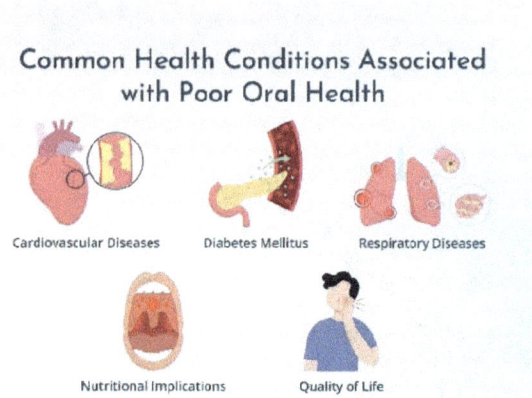

Expertise in Nutritional Assessment

Nutritionists are skilled in assessing the nutritional status of patients with respiratory conditions. This includes evaluating dietary intake, body composition, and biochemical markers to identify nutritional deficiencies and excesses. Proper nutritional assessment is essential for developing individualized nutrition plans that support respiratory health.

Nutrition and Respiratory Health

Optimal nutrition is vital for maintaining respiratory function and overall health. Nutritionists understand the complex relationship between diet and respiratory health, including how certain nutrients can impact lung function, inflammation, and immune response. They provide dietary recommendations that can help manage symptoms and improve quality of life for patients with respiratory conditions.

Developing Individualized Nutrition Plans

Nutritionists develop personalized nutrition plans tailored to the specific needs of patients with respiratory conditions. This includes recommending nutrient-dense foods that provide the necessary vitamins, minerals, and antioxidants to support lung health. They also address issues such as malnutrition, obesity, and other comorbidities that can affect respiratory function.

Education and Counseling

Educating patients about the importance of nutrition in respiratory health is a key responsibility of nutritionists. They provide guidance on healthy eating habits, portion control, and meal planning. Nutritionists also counsel patients on how to manage dietary restrictions and make healthier food choices to support their respiratory health.

Monitoring and Adjusting Nutrition Plans

Nutritionists monitor patients' progress and adjust their nutrition plans as needed to ensure optimal outcomes. This includes tracking changes in weight, body composition, and dietary intake. Nutritionists use this information to make necessary adjustments to the nutrition plan to better meet the patient's needs.

Collaboration with the Healthcare Team

Nutritionists collaborate with physicians, nurses, respiratory therapists, and other healthcare providers to develop and implement comprehensive care plans. Their expertise in nutrition is essential for ensuring that all aspects of the patient's dietary needs are addressed.

Research and Quality Improvement

Many nutritionists are involved in research and quality improvement initiatives aimed at advancing nutritional practices in respiratory care. This includes conducting clinical trials, implementing evidence-based practices, and contributing to the development of clinical guidelines.

Challenges Faced by Nutritionists

Nutritionists face several challenges in their role within the interdisciplinary team:

- Patient Adherence: Ensuring that patients adhere to dietary recommendations can be challenging, especially for those with long-standing eating habits or food preferences.
- Resource Limitations: Limited access to certain foods and nutritional supplements can hinder the ability to provide optimal care.
- Complex Cases: Managing patients with multiple comorbidities and varying nutritional needs requires specialized skills and adaptability.

Enhancing the Role of Nutritionists in Interdisciplinary Care

To enhance the role of nutritionists in interdisciplinary respiratory care, the following strategies can be implemented:

- Ongoing Education and Training: Providing nutritionists with continuing education and training in respiratory care and interdisciplinary practice can enhance their knowledge and skills.
- Supportive Work Environment: Creating a supportive work environment with adequate resources and opportunities for professional development can help nutritionists manage their workload and provide high-quality care.
- Interdisciplinary Collaboration: Encouraging regular interdisciplinary meetings and communication can foster a collaborative culture and improve care coordination.

Nutritionists are vital members of the interdisciplinary respiratory care team, contributing their expertise in dietary management to support respiratory health. Their role in optimizing nutrition and enhancing patient outcomes is essential for delivering comprehensive, patient-centered care. By addressing the challenges they face and enhancing their involvement in interdisciplinary practice, we can improve outcomes for patients with respiratory conditions.

DISCUSSION QUESTIONS

- What role do nutritionists play in addressing dietary concerns and optimizing nutritional intake for patients with respiratory conditions, and how does this contribute to improved respiratory outcomes?
- How can nutritionists collaborate with other members of the interdisciplinary team to develop comprehensive care plans that address both nutritional and respiratory needs?

MODULE FIVE

LESSON ONE: THE ROLE OF SOCIAL WORKERS IN RESPIRATORY CARE

Social workers are essential members of the interdisciplinary team, providing psychosocial support and resources to patients and their families. This lesson explores the role of social workers in

THE SOCIAL WORKER'S ROLE ON HEALTH TEAMS

Social workers are essential to the delivery and design of optimal health care.
- They work on health teams comprised of direct patient-care professionals and as administrators overseeing program planning and implementation.
- Tasks include:
  - goals of the profession of social work.
  - helping clients problem solve and cope with life stressors.
  - Linking individuals with resources, services, and opportunities;
  - Promoting effective and human service systems.
  - Developing and improving social policy.

respiratory care, highlighting their contributions to addressing social determinants of health and improving patient outcomes.

Expertise in Psychosocial Assessment

Social workers are trained in conducting comprehensive psychosocial assessments, identifying factors that may impact a patient's health and well-being. This includes evaluating the patient's emotional, social, and environmental circumstances, as well as their support systems and coping mechanisms.

Emotional and Psychological Support

Respiratory conditions can have a significant emotional and psychological impact on patients and their families. Social workers provide counseling and support to help patients cope with anxiety, depression, and other mental health issues related to their condition. They also offer support to family members, helping them navigate the challenges of caring for a loved one with a chronic respiratory illness.

Resource Coordination

Social workers connect patients and families with resources and services to support their needs. This includes coordinating access to financial assistance, transportation, housing, and other community resources. By addressing these social determinants of health, social workers help to remove barriers to care and improve overall well-being.

Education and Advocacy

Educating patients and families about their rights and available resources is a key responsibility of social workers. They advocate on behalf of patients to ensure they receive the services and support they need. This includes assisting with insurance issues, securing disability benefits, and navigating healthcare systems.

Discharge Planning and Follow-Up

Social workers play a critical role in discharge planning, ensuring that patients have a smooth transition from hospital to home or another care setting. They develop discharge plans that address the patient's medical, social, and emotional needs. Follow-up support is provided to ensure that patients have access to necessary resources and services after discharge.

Collaboration with the Healthcare Team

Social workers collaborate with physicians, nurses, respiratory therapists, and other healthcare providers to develop and implement comprehensive care plans. Their expertise in psychosocial care is essential for addressing the holistic needs of patients and ensuring coordinated, patient-centered care.

Research and Quality Improvement

Many social workers are involved in research and quality improvement initiatives aimed at advancing psychosocial care practices in respiratory health. This includes conducting studies on the impact of social determinants of health, implementing evidence-based interventions, and contributing to the development of clinical guidelines.

Challenges Faced by Social Workers

Social workers face several challenges in their role within the interdisciplinary team:

- Complex Psychosocial Issues: Addressing the complex and multifaceted psychosocial issues of patients with respiratory conditions requires specialized skills and resources.
- Resource Limitations: Limited access to community resources and support services can hinder the ability to provide optimal care.
- Interdisciplinary Communication: Ensuring effective communication and collaboration with other healthcare providers is essential but can be challenging.

Enhancing the Role of Social Workers in Interdisciplinary Care

To enhance the role of social workers in interdisciplinary respiratory care, the following strategies can be implemented:

- Ongoing Education and Training: Providing social workers with continuing education and training in respiratory care and interdisciplinary practice can enhance their knowledge and skills.
- Supportive Work Environment: Creating a supportive work environment with adequate resources and opportunities for professional development can help social workers manage their workload and provide high-quality care.
- Interdisciplinary Collaboration: Encouraging regular interdisciplinary meetings and communication can foster a collaborative culture and improve care coordination.

Social workers are vital members of the interdisciplinary respiratory care team, contributing their expertise in psychosocial support and resource coordination. Their role in addressing social determinants of health and providing emotional and psychological support is essential for delivering comprehensive, patient-centered care. By addressing the challenges they face and enhancing their involvement in interdisciplinary practice, we can improve outcomes for patients with respiratory conditions.

DISCUSSION QUESTIONS

- How do social workers contribute to addressing the psychosocial needs of patients with respiratory conditions, and how does this support interdisciplinary care?
- What strategies can interdisciplinary teams implement to ensure effective collaboration with social workers and maximize the benefits of their expertise in respiratory care?

MODULE SIX

LESSON ONE: IMPLEMENTING INTERDISCIPLINARY CARE IN PRACTICE

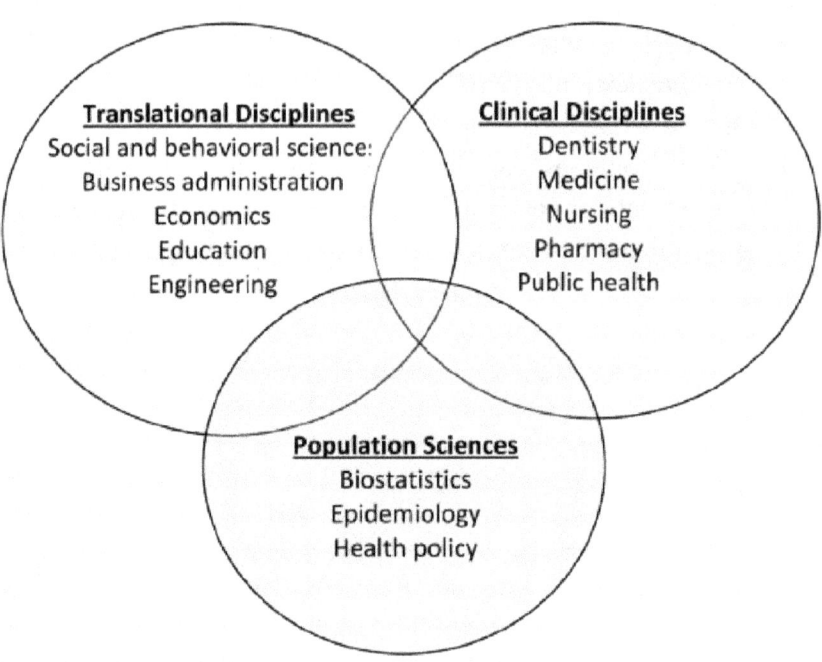

Successfully implementing an interdisciplinary approach to respiratory care requires careful planning, collaboration, and ongoing evaluation. This lesson provides a roadmap for healthcare providers to develop and sustain effective interdisciplinary care teams, highlighting key steps and strategies for implementation.

Building an Interdisciplinary Team

Creating a successful interdisciplinary team involves identifying and recruiting healthcare providers from various disciplines who are committed to collaborative care. Key steps include:

- Identifying Core Team Members: Assemble a team that includes physicians, nurses, respiratory therapists,

pharmacists, physical therapists, nutritionists, social workers, and other relevant professionals.
- Defining Roles and Responsibilities: Clearly define the roles and responsibilities of each team member to ensure that all aspects of patient care are addressed comprehensively.
- Establishing Leadership: Designate a team leader or coordinator who will oversee the team's activities, facilitate communication, and ensure that care plans are implemented effectively.

Developing Interdisciplinary Care Plans

Interdisciplinary care plans are essential for ensuring that all aspects of a patient's care are addressed. Key elements include:

- Comprehensive Assessment: Conduct a thorough assessment of the patient's medical, psychosocial, and functional status to identify their needs and goals.
- Collaborative Goal Setting: Work with the patient and their family to set achievable and meaningful goals that guide the care plan.
- Integrated Care Planning: Develop a care plan that integrates the expertise of all team members, ensuring that interventions are coordinated and complementary.

Enhancing Communication and Collaboration

Effective communication and collaboration are critical for the success of interdisciplinary care. Strategies include:

- Regular Team Meetings: Hold regular interdisciplinary team meetings to discuss patient progress, update care plans, and address any issues or concerns.
- Electronic Health Records (EHRs): Utilize EHRs to facilitate information sharing and ensure that all team members have access to up-to-date patient information.

- Interdisciplinary Rounds: Conduct interdisciplinary rounds where team members visit patients together, discuss care plans, and make real-time adjustments.

Education and Training

Providing ongoing education and training for team members is essential for maintaining high standards of care. Key areas include:

- Interdisciplinary Practice: Offer training on the principles and practices of interdisciplinary care, emphasizing the importance of collaboration and communication.
- Clinical Competencies: Provide continuing education to enhance clinical skills and knowledge in respiratory care and related fields.
- Team-Building Activities: Facilitate team-building activities to strengthen relationships and foster a collaborative team culture.

Evaluating and Improving Care

Continuous evaluation and quality improvement are necessary for sustaining effective interdisciplinary care. Strategies include:

- Outcome Measures: Track patient outcomes to assess the effectiveness of interdisciplinary care and identify areas for improvement.
- Patient Feedback: Gather feedback from patients and families to understand their experiences and identify opportunities for enhancing care.
- Quality Improvement Initiatives: Implement quality improvement initiatives based on data and feedback, and involve team members in the process to ensure buy-in and participation.

Addressing Challenges and Barriers

Implementing interdisciplinary care can present several challenges and barriers. Strategies for addressing these include:

- Resource Allocation: Ensure that adequate resources, including time, staff, and funding, are allocated to support interdisciplinary care.
- Cultural Change: Promote a culture of collaboration and respect among team members, emphasizing the value of interdisciplinary practice.
- Administrative Support: Secure support from healthcare administrators and leaders to advocate for and sustain interdisciplinary care initiatives.

Case Study: Successful Implementation of Interdisciplinary Care

A case study illustrating the successful implementation of interdisciplinary care can provide valuable insights and lessons learned. This case study should highlight:

- The Initial Challenges: Describe the initial challenges faced in implementing interdisciplinary care, such as resistance to change or resource limitations.
- Strategies Used: Outline the strategies used to overcome these challenges, such as team-building activities, education and training programs, and administrative support.
- Positive Outcomes: Highlight the positive outcomes achieved through interdisciplinary care, including improved patient satisfaction, better health outcomes, and enhanced team collaboration.

Implementing an interdisciplinary approach to respiratory care requires careful planning, collaboration, and ongoing evaluation. By building a strong team, developing integrated care plans, enhancing communication, providing education and training, and continuously evaluating care, healthcare providers can deliver comprehensive, patient-centered care. Addressing challenges and barriers through strategic initiatives and fostering a culture of collaboration are essential for sustaining effective interdisciplinary practice and improving outcomes for patients with respiratory conditions.

DISCUSSION QUESTIONS

What are some potential barriers to implementing interdisciplinary care in respiratory health settings, and how can healthcare organizations overcome these barriers?

How can healthcare providers measure the effectiveness of interdisciplinary care in improving patient outcomes and satisfaction in respiratory care settings?

MODULE SEVEN

LESSON ONE: CASE STUDIES AND PRACTICAL APPLICATIONS

The interdisciplinary approach to respiratory care is best understood through practical examples and real-world applications. This lesson presents case studies that illustrate how the collaborative efforts of healthcare providers can lead to improved patient outcomes. Each case study highlights the roles of different team members and the importance of effective communication and coordination.

CASE STUDY 1: CHRONIC OBSTRUCTIVE PULMONARY DISEASE (COPD)

Patient Background:

Mr. Smith, a 68-year-old male with a history of smoking, presents with worsening dyspnea, chronic cough, and frequent exacerbations of COPD.

Interdisciplinary Team:

- Physician: Diagnosed COPD and developed a treatment plan that includes bronchodilators, corticosteroids, and pulmonary rehabilitation.
- Nurse: Monitored Mr. Smith's symptoms, provided education on medication use, and managed follow-up care.
- Respiratory Therapist: Administered respiratory therapies, adjusted ventilator settings during exacerbations, and taught breathing techniques.
- Pharmacist: Conducted medication reconciliation, provided counseling on medication adherence, and monitored for drug interactions.
- Physical Therapist: Designed and supervised an exercise program tailored to Mr. Smith's capabilities, including aerobic and strength training exercises.

- Nutritionist: Developed a nutrition plan to address Mr. Smith's weight loss and optimize his dietary intake for respiratory health.

Outcome:

Through the coordinated efforts of the interdisciplinary team, Mr. Smith's symptoms improved significantly. His exacerbations decreased, he experienced better control of his dyspnea, and his overall quality of life improved. Regular follow-ups and adjustments to his care plan ensured that he remained stable and managed his condition effectively.

CASE STUDY 2: ASTHMA MANAGEMENT IN A PEDIATRIC PATIENT

Patient Background:

Emily, a 10-year-old girl, has a history of asthma with frequent nighttime symptoms and emergency room visits due to exacerbations.

Interdisciplinary Team:

- Physician: Diagnosed asthma, prescribed a long-term control medication plan, and created an asthma action plan.
- Nurse: Educated Emily and her parents on asthma management, proper inhaler technique, and symptom monitoring.
- Respiratory Therapist: Conducted spirometry tests, provided breathing exercises, and monitored Emily's lung function.
- Pharmacist: Ensured appropriate medication use, offered counseling on potential side effects, and checked for adherence to the medication regimen.
- Physical Therapist: Developed a physical activity plan that included exercises to improve lung capacity and endurance without triggering asthma symptoms.
- Nutritionist: Provided dietary recommendations to help manage potential asthma triggers and support overall health.

Outcome:

With the comprehensive, interdisciplinary approach, Emily's asthma was brought under control. She experienced fewer nighttime symptoms and emergency visits, her lung function improved, and she was able to participate in school and physical activities without limitations. The team's ongoing support and education empowered Emily and her family to effectively manage her asthma.

CASE STUDY 3: RESPIRATORY FAILURE IN A POSTOPERATIVE PATIENT

Patient Background:

Mrs. Johnson, a 55-year-old female, developed respiratory failure following a major abdominal surgery.

Interdisciplinary Team:

- Physician: Managed her medical care, prescribed mechanical ventilation, and oversaw the transition to weaning.
- Nurse: Monitored her vital signs, managed her pain, and provided postoperative care.
- Respiratory Therapist: Managed ventilator settings, performed weaning trials, and provided airway clearance techniques.
- Pharmacist: Monitored and adjusted medications, including antibiotics and analgesics, to prevent complications and manage pain.
- Physical Therapist: Implemented early mobilization protocols, including bed exercises and gradual ambulation.
- Nutritionist: Developed a nutrition plan to support healing, including high-protein meals to aid in recovery.

Outcome:

The interdisciplinary team's coordinated care led to a successful recovery for Mrs. Johnson. She was weaned off mechanical ventilation, her respiratory function stabilized, and she regained mobility through physical therapy. Nutritional support helped in her overall recovery, leading to a discharge plan that included continued rehabilitation and follow-up care.

Practical Applications and Lessons Learned

These case studies highlight several key aspects of interdisciplinary respiratory care:

- Effective Communication: Clear and consistent communication among team members is essential for coordinated care. Regular meetings and updates ensure that everyone is informed about the patient's status and care plan.
- Patient-Centered Approach: Tailoring care to meet the individual needs of each patient improves outcomes and enhances patient satisfaction. Understanding the patient's goals and involving them in the care process is crucial.
- Collaboration and Role Clarity: Each team member brings unique expertise to the table. Recognizing and valuing these contributions ensures that all aspects of patient care are addressed comprehensively.
- Continuous Improvement: Ongoing education, training, and quality improvement initiatives help healthcare providers stay updated on best practices and new developments in respiratory care.
- Holistic Care: Addressing not only the medical but also the psychological, nutritional, and physical needs of patients leads to better health outcomes and quality of life.

The interdisciplinary approach to respiratory care, as illustrated by these case studies, demonstrates the importance of collaboration, communication, and patient-centered care. By leveraging the expertise of various healthcare professionals, we can provide comprehensive, effective, and compassionate care to patients with respiratory conditions.

DISCUSSION QUESTIONS

- How do the case studies presented in this lesson illustrate the effectiveness of interdisciplinary care in managing various respiratory conditions, and what lessons can be learned from these cases?
- What are some key takeaways from the practical applications discussed in this lesson, and how can healthcare organizations apply these principles to improve interdisciplinary respiratory care in their own settings?

CONCLUSION

The exploration of interdisciplinary respiratory care underscores the critical importance of collaboration, communication, and comprehensive patient-centered approaches in managing respiratory conditions effectively. Through the collective expertise of physicians, nurses, respiratory therapists, pharmacists, physical therapists, nutritionists, and social workers, interdisciplinary teams can address the multifaceted needs of patients with respiratory ailments.

Understanding respiratory anatomy and physiology forms the foundational knowledge upon which interdisciplinary care plans are built. This knowledge informs the tailored interventions and treatments necessary for managing diverse respiratory disorders. Principles of interdisciplinary practice guide teams in fostering a collaborative environment where each member's expertise is valued and utilized to its fullest potential.

By embracing interdisciplinary approaches, healthcare providers can better meet the complex needs of patients with respiratory conditions, ultimately leading to improved health outcomes and enhanced quality of life.

REFERENCES

Arnold, M. (2018). *Collaborative Practices in Respiratory Therapy. Journal of Interprofessional Care.*

Adams, E. (2019). *Physical Therapy Interventions for Respiratory Conditions: A Comprehensive Review. Journal of Cardiopulmonary Rehabilitation and Prevention.*

Brown, J. (2018). *Interdisciplinary Teamwork in Pulmonary Rehabilitation: A Practical Guide. Respiratory Care.*

Clark, A. (2017). *Effective Communication Strategies for Interdisciplinary Respiratory Care Teams. Journal of Interprofessional Education & Practice*

Davis, R. (2019). *Interdisciplinary Approach to Respiratory Care: Challenges and Opportunities. Respiratory Medicine.*

Garcia, S. (2020). *The Role of Pharmacists in Interdisciplinary Respiratory Care. Pharmacy Today.*

Johnson, L. (2017). *Comprehensive Nutritional Management in Respiratory Health. Journal of Nutrition and Dietetics.*

Smith, K. (2016). Psychosocial Support in Respiratory Care: *The Role of Social Workers. Journal of Social Work in Health Care.*

www.ingramcontent.com/pod-product-compliance
Lightning Source LLC
Chambersburg PA
CBHW070442010526
44118CB00014B/2151